Small Towns is an accomplished collection of free-verse and structured poetry exploring the relationship between people and place, the human condition against the natural world.

Melissa Watts shines a light on the unsaid. She picks the scab of small-town tensions, then unflinchingly aims her bow at social injustice, tipping her hat to the feminist poets who have come before her.

Small Towns

Small Towns

Poems of people and place

Melissa Watts

nine cups

Copyright © Melissa Watts, 2022

This book is copyright. Apart from any fair dealing for the purposes of study and research, criticism, review or as otherwise permitted under the Copyright Act., no part may be reproduced by any process without written permission. Inquiries should be made to the publisher.

First published in 2022
Published by Nine Cups Press
Ballarat, Victoria, 3350
ninecupspress.com

ISBN: 9780646847924 : Paperback
9780646847931 : ebook – epub

A catalogue record for this book is available from the National Library of Australia

For

A	K	F	Q	P	D	S	E
C	H̶	F	A	J̶	E	L̶	L
B̶	E̶	N̶	J̶	A̶	M̶	I̶	N̶
A	N̶	E	C	M̶	F	L̶	P
Z	R̶	V	W	E̶	Z	L̶	O
H	Y̶	L	Q	S̶	Q	I̶	C
F	S	J	D	B	L	A̶	V
I	V	M	U	F	I	N̶	B

Contents

Author's note i

Summer

In the Beginning 1
Ancient Breezes 2
Cartographies 3
She and Him 4
George and the Vegans 5
The Worm Farm 8
The Wattle Tree 9
Nan's Fowlers Vacola 10
Walhalla 12
Coastal Town 13
The Beach 14
Cloud Shadow Cinquain 15
Afternoon at the Dam 16
Mother's Day 17

Autumn

Main Street 23
Aerial 24
Rainbow Lorikeets 25
Cockatoos 26

A Fraction of a Mouse 27

Just Passing Through 28

Grog 30

in praise of click and collect... 32

Tasmania 2018 36

Mindfulness 38

The Escape 39

The Gloaming 40

Winter

How to paint a sigh 47

Freezing 48

Waiting for the morning school bus 49

Pastoral 50

Haiku for Bert 52

Winter Solstice 53

Grief – who wore it best? 54

Migration 55

A King Amongst Cacti 56

Oh, Camelia 57

Knowing 58

lactation + consultant = Lactation Consultant 59

If the town had a flavour 60

Spring

Inland Sea 67
Seeds 68
Djerrinallum (Mount Elephant) 69
Bees – a love letter 70
Cinquain for Chickens 71
Stock Crossing 72
Home 73
The Word Search 74
Gifts 76
The Secret 77
Scones 78
The C.W.A. 79
What would Kate Jennings do? 80

Acknowledgements 82

About the Author 83

Author's note

It is the job of a writer to tell a story, to record a scene, to capture emotion. It is the job of the reader to interpret that story, to imagine that scene, to feel that emotion. The two, the writer and the reader, work in tandem. The writer trusts that the crumbs they leave will be collected. But there are times when a writer can't say it all. The meter of the poem might dictate that words be removed. There might be sections discarded to make the poem rest easy in the ear and on the tongue. Some fragments catch light and others don't, but that doesn't mean that they are not there. They are simply waiting for their reader. The challenge of the reader is to bring light to a section that a poet hasn't illuminated. To polish a rough gem.

There will be times when genders, identities, cultures and locations are named, and there are times when you can interpret as you wish. My challenge to you is to cast your mind wide – some stories are not mine to tell.

Likewise, while I have used the four seasons of the Gregorian calendar as a structure to this collection, I acknowledge that there are many customary seasonal descriptions, so feel free to read in any order you like.

Enjoy.

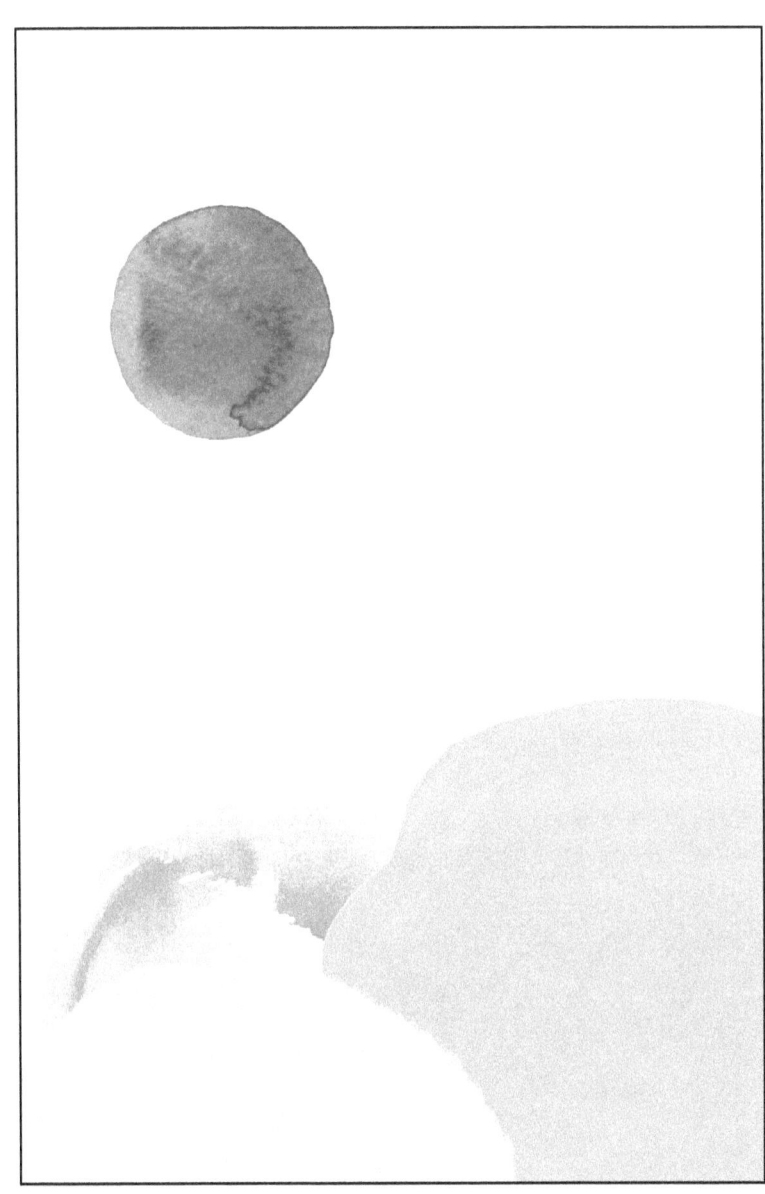

Summer

In the Beginning

in   the   beginning

         < < the beginning > >

           a wilderness of stars

                                     still

                 knows the beginning

    dawn

           remembers

                 the beginning

                               we
                               breathe
                               air
                               from
                               the
                               beginning

Ancient Breezes

This night's ancient breath —

                    its immemorial heat

        has touched the earth before,

run
its ponderous paw
        slow
           low
                  against the earth,

      absorbed the sun's heat,

lain
      in wait
            for insignificant
                            s
                            t a r
                            s

then   s t r e t c h e d   its
        b e l l y
                up

            a gift for the

                        m
                      o   o
                        n

Cartographies

small towns
moor to
road-jetties
enclosed by
paddock stitched
to paddock
stitched to paddock
netted like
effulgent fish - hundreds
of kilometers
from a coast

        triodia scrub
        bristly wallaby-grass
        regain footholds
        between steel tracks
        forgotten by rail
        an occasional
        eucalypt - older
        than anything here
        houses its
        own microcosm

                tracts of water
                journeys an ancient
                path in its own time
                ripe birdsong explodes
                heavies the air
                then water
                and song
                vanish for
                another
                thousand
                moons

She and Him

It's sausages on Tuesdays, but
she's made vegan fajitas, hot
sauce turns his nose. Elbows
on the table, arms tattooed
with roses she can't afford
to colour. He examines
her face, searches for the
familiarity he'd heard
in her laugh during last
nights *Simpsons* repeat.

When she'd called, *Geoff,*
can I use the spare room?
he'd wondered when she'd stopped
calling him Dad. *It's your room*, he said.
Thirteen years, she replied, then
something about getting back on her feet.

She'd laughed at posters gone
but still the map-embossed desk.
I've been to London, she leaned
above the world, *Berlin*
is magic. He left
her to it.

After dinner they walk the terrier.
She holds the lead, talks
about the road into town,
and nothing ever changing.
He wants to say he's glad she's home,
when he thinks about why she might
have left he feels sick, *We*
need some rain, he says.

George and the Vegans

I

Neither gawking nor spying,
George inspects the street through
his sheers. They've returned on bikes,
from the ridiculously named *farmers market,*
by the looks of the rhubarb.

Two women, living together,
with no car, but a dog
they refer to as their fur-baby.
Both vegans, they told him,
when they dropped off excess tomatoes,
and he tried to give them eggs.

Sixty years he's lived in this house,
and never
        has he heard it
               called 'post-war retro'.

II

George can't remember their names.
Sheryl next door stirs sugar into
his tea and tells him that
Meagan teaches at the primary school,
and *specialises* in autism.
Rebecca *works from home.*

He gets the *Herald-Sun* delivered
each morning, so he knows about vegans,
and autism, and women who live together.
He bites his Scotch Finger and wonders
if they're also 'millennials'.
Sheryl raises her eyebrow and admits to a plan
to lure Rebecca to the Finance sub-committee
of the Lioness club. According to Sheryl,
it's nice to have new faces in town.

III

The power goes out during
A Current Affair, leaving
George in his armchair, with the
blue light hiss of the gas heater.
He waits a few minutes, tightens
his dressing gown cord, congratulates
himself for installing sturdy curtains
thirty years ago, then decides to
find a torch.

He is shoulder-deep in the cupboard
under the sink when a knock at the
door weakens his bowels. An adrenaline
rush, a knee shake, and the knowledge that he
is an old man easily robbed. Another knock,
he sits on the lino in the dark,
waiting
then realises
that thieves don't knock.

At the door, a young woman smiles at him,
with a mobile phone that is also a torch.
'You're coming with me George, we have
Scrabble and cake, and I'll walk you home
at 10 if the power's not back.'
George stands on the threshold,
in slippers and gown,
and smiles back.
It's not her fault she's bossy,
all vegans are like that.

The Worm Farm

Up the back behind the peach tree,
he keeps his fishing worms
safe in an old bath, under a sheet
of corrugated iron -
a mortared brick the weight.

It mirage-shimmers
       like a promise,
the day's dry heat rises off the concrete,
a blue OMO bucket dances in his grip,
as he limps,
       in his iconic way,
his small-town-famous,
bandy legged way,
down the rubber matted back step,
       past the hill's hoist.

There's a smooth metallic sigh
as he slides the iron back -
into steamy air he tips
scraps down one end,
scoops the worms into
their temporary stay from the other.

       Enough,
for him and a mate, although
Romulus always brings his own bait, to
lure eel rather than redfin.

The Wattle Tree

Inside the wattle tree,
manning the lookout is
only for the brave.

He's always there first,
faster on the BMX,
and she always uses her bike stand.

He climbs fast,
knows the branches,
eager to claim the captain's seat
and wave to the approaching train.
Soft under foot, the fallen leaves
lie ankle-deep, pushed into a mound,
for the girl to sit and wish
she was bold enough
to climb.

Nan's Fowlers Vacola

Like a round old hen,
warm with dirt and mid-day lethargy,
the old brown tub has presence.

I eye it down in defiance –
You'll not intimidate me,
with your well-worn guidebook
and external thermometer in Fahrenheit.
Don't let the bottle's touch, she warned
as I loaded my car with old boxes
of jars and lids.

There's a sense of physics, biology,
words like preservation, sterilisation, bacteria,
But, if Nan can do it…

I remove bricks from the garden bed edge
to arrange a stand on the laundry floor.
I measure water, sugar and double-check,
cram and poke, squeak fruit against glass, fearful
of bruising although she told me not to be.
Sleek, is a word for cats and fast-talking men,
and now for the movement of sugar-syrup
over downy apricot.

I straight-jacket lids to jars,
bed them gently in water,
ten golden moons in a pond.
I put the lid on and wait in silence.
Then eventually, a sigh of steam,
bubble released from its boil.

Mercury rises in my humid laundry,
I do the maths again in my head,
time and temperature lace fingers, couple.

Waiting in the kitchen, I pour tea from the pot
and wonder about the other women who've bottled here.
In the garden there are ten fruit trees –
I'm not the first drink tea while I look out the window and wait.

Months later I knife-crack the seal on the first jar.
The champagne zing of summer's apricots
flies up my nose
and I feel
like I'm floating -
I pick up the phone and call Nan.

Walhalla

In 1882 the miners finished their oval,
excavated thirty meters off the nearest mountain,
to make a flat space large enough
for a game of cricket.

Picks and shovels and barrow only,
the chips echoed through the valley.

750 meters above the town,
the steep hike itself is enough
to exhaust the opposition before
a single ball has been bowled.

Coastal Town

summer brings the flocks –
seagull   plover   seaweed   tourist

inundating / swarming

chocking up caravans
guy roping tents
flattening grass
smoke smudging air
dropping in on waves
fishing the cape
buying all the pies
bins abundant with empty stubbies

stealing the hot day's length
from locals who wait
for the retreat a few days
before school term.

The Beach

You've been to the beach once.
Intolerable.
Too bright, too loud,
sandy, no shade.
Scrubby brush,
Plovers who nest,
Penguins who roost
in the only vegetation,
Dogs who lay turds to weather and dry,
the dank dead smell of rotting seaweed,
the paddle out in water full of God-knows what,
just to be pushed back to shore,
or swept out to oblivion.
The lying in the sun,
not doing a single productive thing,
the skin cancer, the skin cancer,
the sand that sticks to sunscreen,
sticks to underwear,
sticks to car seats and bed sheets.
The impolite roar of the ocean
so the whole trip is spent yelling,
the glare that burns out your retinas.
Sure you could eat fresh fish,
but what could you grow?

Cloud Shadow Cinquain

shadow
clouds across the
dust, shifting lacuna,
worthless fluff, no promise of rain —
liars

Afternoon at the Dam

Yabbie nets drip from the branch, catch
sunlight through leaf lacuna,
their damp spread evaporates,
leaving pock marks in the dust.

A wet dog rolls in happiness,
on dried cow pats, smooths itself
against the earth, turns belly up
to the sun. Kids smear

mud on bare chests, laughter
bounces across water, conjures
cries from irrelevant birds startled
into flight in the distance.

Mother's Day

It roars like surf - that smoke mass. Tall
flame indistinct from its neighbour,
the ancient land betrays us rapidly. Breathy
howls clog ears, crawl down throats uninvited,
grate cornea with acrid heat.

I grip pink/soot fingers, white knuckled. Little
hands that I created, my love and terror entwined
with theirs.   We run.

And then an eye catch.

Black panic that mirrors mine - she hops once,
then off, another way, into scrub with her
softly angled joey mound.

Autumn

Main Street

Paint-chipped along groove and tongue,
veiled with dust, the locked doors
attempt a landscape camouflage.
Balconied pubs, millinered with decorative
lace and brooches of faded ladies lounge signs,
sigh from their wooden cellar-doors,
cold gossip of the past.

The population of twenty-five, don't hear it,
they tune their ears to weather forecasts and
focus on potholes in roads. A couple of elms
survive on the Avenue of Honour.

In a nest of dry grass and iron
fencing the old school building sits.
The bell's skeleton-scaffold, tanned with rust,
winks at the cyclone wire bordering
what was once a tennis court,
an incline in the dirt, the grave
of a cricket pitch, a barely visible embankment –
the ghost of a train line.

Aerial

corrugated iron
roof rectangles
catch sun
and glisten
upward like
teeth

   t
      h
         r
            e
               a
                  d
                     s

                        of flattened   ground
                               web   between
                              dual   lines
                               for   vehicles
                                             single
                                             for
                                             sheep
                                   then

                             peter

                      o
                  u
                t

     a brown dam
    haloed by mud
    darkens into the
    space like a day
     three bruise

Rainbow Lorikeets

Rainbow Lorikeets rally
like it's the London blitz -
from the tree,

                round the yard,

and back.

The flash of colour,
engine-wing purr
and shrill call so loud
the chickens bunker.
They camouflage
in the bright green
leaves before the autumnal
turn hurls them from the yard,
and it's feast of fruit, into
the state forest down the valley,
and I am left jealous - pecking
away at a keyboard,
like an ineffective wren.

Cockatoos

Cockatoos are out today,
fucking me off like the little
beady-eyed pricks
that they are, grabbing
at the ground
with their reptilian claws,
cracking the apples
just to pick the seeds,
eyeballing me upside down
as they swing,
the fat bastards,
and me, stuck on the porch,
red tartan blanket
tucked across knees,
grey tartan dressing gown
over blue tartan pyjamas
like some kind
of Scottish Christmas biscuit box
waiting for her to come out with
a luke-warm tea and a straw.

A Fraction of a Mouse

Gumboot heeled in chook shit,
jacket zipped to chin, each morning
the traps are checked. Crouched

against the grain dispenser,
she dislodges the plastic box, lays
it in an old mop bucket.

The side of the shed, verandah steps,
water tank, she gathers
the black tombs. Plastic key

into plastic key-hole, unlocks
the box, exposes jaw-traps, firm
against their soft catch.

Fur as meek as dandelion pappus,
ears paper-transparent,
minute claws curled. But

today, fluff and dark pink sinew,
that once lead to something
falls from the trap.

Where is the rest, eaten? Escaped?
A fraction of a mouse, a portion, a puff
to contemplate over morning coffee.

Just Passing Through

He sits on the park bench
to catch his breath,
rests his few shopping bags at his feet,
and watches the family.

The mother launches off monkey bars,
two small boys follow,
caught in her imaginary wake,
their laughter bouncing like
her quick ankles,
as she gathers energy,
takes movement
for granted.

He once conjured energy
through air too – dividing matter
with a leather ball, running, arching,
hurling a spin-bowl to change
its trajectory.

The father swing-pushes a toddler,
open mouthed, billowed hair, air
against cheeks, the old man
remembers the thrill of a billy cart -
God, it must be eighty years ago -
with a brother long dead.

The woman runs laps between
imaginary markers. Her boys follow,
laughing but determined,
they issue a cry of victory
when she lies on the grass and they have won.

He longs for the pleasure of movement,
for a lengthened spine, a knee without creak,
a smile and a wave is all he can muster,
when they walk past him to the car,
loaded with suitcases and pillows -
they are just passing through.

Grog

In ~~Canberra / the nation's capital~~
our nation's capital
men,
eat steak for lunch,
slide red fibres,
from between pearlescent teeth with
unchipped thumb nails and discuss
~~rural Australia / regional Australians~~
The Bush.

They congratulate themselves on
reaching the term
~~mateship / looking out for your mates~~
resilience,
in their effort to
~~battle / fight~~
combat
mental health issues.
Funding ~~services~~ groups that
focus on ~~sobriety / alcoholism~~
alcohol awareness
is unnecessary, because ~~the taxes,~~
the workers - a kick to the teeth for those
in the vineyards earning a
~~fair / decent~~
honest living.
And who doesn't love a beer?
Political suicide to go up against
~~a larrikin, / an icon~~
an Aussie way of life
for no good reason.
Not to mention the
~~sheilas / the girls~~

women
who need their 'mummy-wine',
the 'cheeky chardy' - at least
they don't take it out in fist fights,
and by God they
~~cash up / spend big~~
support
the market by the millions.

Mental health is
~~easy to fund~~
on trend.
Suicide is
~~skyrocketing / out of control~~
at concerning levels,
the bush is
~~not supporting themselves /~~
~~has dropped the ball~~
is in need of assistance.
And the country is built on
~~sucking it up / being a man~~
mateship.

We're here to
~~throw money at the problem /~~
~~get to the next election~~
support our mates in the bush.
Programs for the blokes. The
ladies always talk it through.
We'll pay a prominent
~~Psychologist/ Mental Health Practitioner~~
Footballer.

in praise of click and collect

just to get here you've hauled your arse out of bed,
breastfed the baby, cerealed the toddler,
coincided the drive with the nap,
driven forty five minutes, breastfed in the carpark,
strapped the baby to you like a parachute. now,
the arched-back toddler refuses the trolley seat,
and you need to get out before someone needs a poo,
or just does a poo, before your frayed edges unravel even more.

let's start with the fruit and veg, everyone needs
to eat more. are the grapes sprayed?
        put those oranges back -
too many food miles on oranges from california,
do strawberries have needles or is that old news now?
herbs are so expensive, wrapped in plastic,
you should plant some, but coriander is a prick of a thing,
and just reminds you of overseas holidays you can't take

then

an old lady pats your baby,
gives you unrequested opinions,
like dogshit wrapped in flaming newspaper, tells
you he's on a good wicket, that mummy
must have the good stuff with a weight like that,
comments on the toddler's red hair,
and you don't have the energy to say that both
fat-shaming and commenting on someone's
appearance is no longer acceptable, so you
clench-jaw-smile and keep walking,
and the music

<< mariah—carey >>
<< mariah—fucking—carey >>
<< dreamlover come rescue me... >>

they target the music in these places, you know,
you saw it in a doco once, when you could do things
          like watch docos,
and the toddler's a coeliac, the toddler's a coeliac, the toddler's a
coeliac, all the vomits and the vomits and the vomits
and the drs and the drs and the drs and the blood tests
and the cameras down the gullets. and it was just the beginning as
you clutch every packet, read every item,
google-check ingredients, with the thought
that she probably won't eat the $7 bread
as you put it in the trolley, because she has 'food trauma',
because you poisoned her with gluten over and over
because her first solids were weetbix, because, because. and the
multivitamins contain gluten and if you lived in a city you
could go somewhere else to buy others,
and why are chips and hotdogs fine
but rice bubbles and cornflakes not?

<< m-people m-people >>
<< movin on up movin on up >>

are the coffee beans rainforest alliance? all queens coffee,
all female workers, yes to that, in it goes, and the tea,
thank god for fair trade mr dilmah, (who is really
called mr fernandez) look at his face, we love him.
the baked beans - packed here,
      but are they grown here?
and what about the sodium, sodium, sodium,
noodles with palm oil can stay on the shelf,
you've been to borneo,

seen the plantations with your own eyes,
fed the homeless orangutans.
this rice is grown in a naturally dry area, irrigation rice,
leave it on the shelf, arborio, jasmine, short grain, sushi,
long grain, what the fuck, there was only one rice
when we were kids
and we survived
        but you can't have thai with arborio.

fuck! don't touch that, don't touch that,
nearly there, nearly there, get up off the floor,
if you give her your phone people will judge
        let her cry.
quinoa – superfood for coeliacs
but aren't the affluent westerners making it hard for bolivians to
afford their own crops? fuckin hipsters,
leave it to the coeliacs please. are we over-fishing?
or is tuna fine? does the salmon have pink die?
the cereal is full of sugar, porridge for everyone,
except the coeliac- or do we all go gluten free,
and avoid cross contamination? avoid the soft drink aisle,
        a whole fucking aisle to itself
pet food, that's right, you take care of six souls, not four
and you won't be buying a dog or cat ever again.
the trolley is too full
but its one shop a month and it needs to be big.
eggs are free range - why do they even bother with battery
anymore, so cruel, you should buy them from those kids at the
roadside stall, but you can't leave your kids in the car, what if
there was an accident, if you park and then....
STOP

        << christina—aguilera >>
        << words can't bring me down... >>

unless it's *i'm hungry*
those two words will bring you down
they'll bring you right fucking down if they're said
by a coeliac toddler in public, let me tell you.
microplastics, microplastics, microplastics in body wash, straight
down the drain, palm oil in shampoo, argan oil? who knows?
detergent that will get stains out but will it kill
the ocean, make the kids breathe toxins fresh from the bib and
their modern cloth bamboo nappies?

in the freezer section
your post baby body (whatever the fuck that means)
makes arse print love hearts on the doors
as they cold-slap you playfully on the rear – ahhh,
remember the playful arse-slap? now a row of freezer love heart
arse prints follows you down the aisle
as you try to remember if the chip mob are back paying their
farmers a fair price. cheese, boutique or mass produced, soft,
firm, blue, orange, local, imported, pizza, shredded, sliced,
economy family priced, how much is milk a litre, is the farmer
getting a good deal, but the anthropocene? should
we have cow's milk or soy milk, who in this family decides?
                       you do!   you do!
you decide what your family will do to the planet
        and their bodies, ha!
what good are strong bones with no planet to house them on?
sow stall free pork, free range chicken, grass-fed beef
should we even be eating meat?
get through the check out

fuck the reusable bags

just get back to the car for a cry.

Tasmania 2018

To get an abortion you need to travel.
You need to leave the state. *You* need to somehow get
a credit card, book a flight, get a bus to an airport,
wait at the airport without being recognised, fly to the
mainland, find a hotel, get to the hotel, get out of the hotel
go to the clinic, fill in the papers, do the counselling,
have the procure, get back to the hotel,
recover in the hotel, get to the airport, fly,
get a bus from the airport, without being recognised.
You need to sort this out, you need to not tell your parents,
you need to think this through, you need to know how to pay,
you need to do it now, you need to not wait.

poem in which mum of three kids with health
issues checks her letterbox in the late
afternoon sun and opens the
annual letter telling her how
much superannuation
she needs before
retirement

slump

Mindfulness

it's the sound of the
cornflake clutching her sock,
off the floor that no one else ever
sweeps. it's heat on her forearms from
the overfilled sink. it's the dancing on the
verge of tears for hours, then deciding on dinner.
it's the incessant cheer of a cartoon soundtrack on repeat
punctured
by a fight, a bite, a run down the hall. it's the roar in her
head. it's the toddler tears that need fixing. now. it's
the over-boiling rice. it's the baby's nappy.
it's finding the joy. it's remembering to
breathe. it's being in the moment
but the moment needs to
fuck right off

The Escape

dusty-sandaled in the park,
the mother invents waves,

her daughter grips the life buoy
swing, face an open sail, squeals

of terror-delight, an imagined
tempest forces eyes to squint.

a seabird lands escaping treacherous
winds, and is fed a fish,

penguins climb aboard and are told to
hold on, a sunhat is lost to the squall.

waves rise higher with each shriek, more
fish are eaten, whales waved to -

thoughts of dank towels requiring
washing whisk into the grey clouds.

email to-dos bob like lost cargo, bills
slip out through the net with each push,

this miracle goes unnoticed by a nanna,
fielding her noisy grandson off the slide, but

back at home, the mother is recompensed
with stickers on hands and a hearty nap.

The Gloaming

slowly, gently and completely against
her will, the night folded, shifted
against the day like a sigh. she saw
through the gloaming the softness
of things – the trees against the paddocks
lost their definition, the birds were lost
to the leaves. unprepared for the vicissitude,
the succession into the dark, the cold
in the lung, she rallied against the
diffusion of her own heart -
not ready to settle into the night.

Winter

How to paint a sigh

Inspired by David Moore,
Untitled (Landscape with Water)

Eucalyptus scent
across water in the
movement of morning's vapour.
White on grey -
a shore which makes
the sound of brush
stroke upon canvas.
Slow waves, the shape
and speed of a contented sigh.
It's a cold filling of lung to the brim,
a warm exhalation into the dawn.

Freezing

Chiselling
frost from windscreen,
its intricate patterns,
toes fiery in boots. The wiper scrape
triggers spine goosebumps,
a clenched jaw, and thoughts
on life in a temperature-controlled house –
a heating system chugging to life before dawn,
heated towel rails, sashays from
hall to garage to temperature
controlled car, to the office, the indoor gym,
back to the car, garage, home,
to the electric blanket in bed --
not once breathing anything as perfect,
and as pure,
as this.

Waiting for the morning school bus

fog
bright white
against dark silhouettes
unequal shapes, sizes
diverse as dreams,
they ground-stomp, urge
warm blood to cold toes,
fold arms into fierce shields
against bony chests and exhale
vaporous clouds
like worship.

a herd
indeterminate
in the luminescent air, they low
with familiarities of the years,
and turn toward where
the road should be, in search
of headlights, thinking
of the warmth of the seat and
not yet considering beyond -
of who in the group will be
the first to leave.

Pastoral

Fog tugs reluctantly
above the dark shape of eucalypts
crowning the hill,
that he greets as his oldest friend.

There is nothing wrong with his vision.

From the verandah he checks for fairy wrens,
pulls a spoon slowly through tea
with hands calloused from a lifetime.

His lungs fill with that pure cold.

At least they have tea, he thinks,
pushing away the thought of the soup-air
he inhaled on the tour.

Jewels of dew light fence wire
and webs, potholes on the track
brim reflected grey -
somebody else can fill them.

He thinks about eyelashes he has known.

The flutter of a feeding newborn, a tear-logged
child, the inconsequential nothingness of
a dead lamb covered in frost.

And hers, on those last few days.

His daughter will arrive for him soon,
his son hiding in the nightmare of a city,
a desk job, and children who 'do' karate.

He waits, still, for the fairy wrens,
the little jester pairs, and ignores
the stock that span back from the house,
pretends he doesn't know the softness of the join
from mouth to cheek of a proud ram.

Haiku for Bert

He knits coats for goats,
vests for abandoned souls to
keep warm near the heart.

Winter Solstice

warm sun through
tractor windscreen like
his mother's full palm
against his puckered cheek,
frost melted into soil, bright blue
sky, he can blame
the tears on the glare.

Grief – who wore it best?

In the battle of,
'Grief: Who Wore it Best?'
they were pitted against each other,
teenaged adversaries, a battle for the ages.
He clutched the hammer of stoicism,
in front of their grandparents,
but a hot-flash to anger at school.
She, the vacant stare of contemplation,
the surveying of what was left.

But their mother trumped them both.

She tamed it, ran her hand down
the quivering flank,
felt the heat, the protruding vein,
whispered in its ear, held
out a treat on her flat palm, then
turned her whip on the estate agent
when he slid his card across the
table, a respectful month after
the funeral, with an offer to move
the farm along. Her unbroken stare
when she informed him
that his performance
on this red carpet would dictate
the long-term success of her children, flicked
the grief back onto the man with
his ironed shirt and price projection.

Migration

He started by googling the trees.
At the heart of it all,
if he sat with it long enough,
he could diagnose grief -
for a home that still exists
without him in it.

In the India of his childhood
a large mango tree grew at the
end of the road. At night,
he uses street view,
to visit the tree. Over the years
streets have been paved, gutters laid,
yellow and black, yellow and black
but the tree remains.

He walks the road to the temple,
searches the screen for his mother's
voice, the quiver of beauty in her poetry,
the millennia-scent of the street,
the colour in the music.

Here only the sky has colour —
when it wants — his own children's
voices are as flat and dry as the landscape.

He knows he shouldn't compare —
it's been forty-five years but the
older he gets the more
his mind returns
to the mango tree
at the end of the street.

A King Amongst Cacti

In the craft room,
on shelves designed for
much larger things, sit
stout jars filled with oddities.
There's blonde fur plucked
from a brush belonging to a dog
now dead, seed pods that look like
goblins, skeletal-leaf fairy wings.

For my craft, she explains. Late
morning sun heralds a desk
of half-finished projects,
unadvanced since
the granddaughters last visit.
Muffin's whiskers, the old woman leans
on her walking stick, points to a dusty jar,
while the cat rubs its flank on a chair leg.
I chopped them while she was sleeping,
a few from each side, good
for the broom on a Beatrix Potter Mrs Mouse.

In the bedroom a rivalry of well groomed
teddies vie for space on the pillow top. Outside
aviaries and turtle ponds wait
for pets long gone, birdfeeders
weather near worn paths.
Did you meet Harry?
In the lip-to-lip kitchen window
plant pots a dead grasshopper
stands, crisp, translucent,
regally petrified.
I keep him because he doesn't eat much.

Oh, Camelia

That tree is hanging on – on its last legs
and you wish it would just die, its mournful reminder
each morning when the curtains are opened is suffocating.
Each leaf that drops, one step closer to the grave –
or the compost heap, as the case may be. But then
it musters up some buds, a sickly few
just to forge the thought that it will push through,
that its position in the decorative hedge,
a la English formal garden,
a la Chelsea flower show,
is worthwhile. It pings thoughts
of collective responsibility
back through the window like a slingshot pebble -
that it's equal to its siblings, that it's worth its place,
that perhaps *you* shouldn't have planted an English tree
in an Australian garden. It squeezes
the guilt from you like a nanna with a flannel,
and you
just wish
it would
hurry the
fuck up
and die
so you can buy a replacement before the siblings
grow too big, so you don't need to be reminded
every morning when you open the curtains
that you are an arsehole.

Knowing

rainbow flags unfurl on the screen
breakfast television hosts with
puckered mouths use new terms –
kick them along like bleached driftwood.

she chews the words over,
tries them on for size,
words she didn't use in 1958
when her brother left.

wandering soul,
they'd said back then,
convincing themselves
he was looking for adventure.

the town was too small
for his wonder,
their home

lacking.

lactation + consultant = Lactation Consultant

across the district
        from plump breast
          to plump breast
she pokes ripe tissue into wide
mouths in search of the perfect latch
stretches thumb and forefinger demonstrating
ideal suction circumference optimal milk retrieval
minimal nipple damage talks mastitis to men who understand
from animal husbandry refuses cups of tea and small talk reminds
that breast is best rattles statistics like an old lady shaking dry food
for a hungry cat pulls out scales and disposable paper measuring
tapes fills in government issued books dispenses full colour
pamphlets with big font helpline numbers looks for signs
of abuse keeps to strictly 30 minutes
eases her arse back into her car
heads off to the
next breast

If the town had a flavour

if you could fit
this town in your mouth,

    would you
    hold it gently between thumb and forefinger,
    intently observe its elements of composition,
    gently lay it on your tongue, press
    softly against the roof of your mouth, eyes closed?

    would you
    angle it deftly, strait between the thick back molars,
    press hard and continue to bite so not one part touches
    a taste bud, swallow it quickly, unforgivingly, to the pit
    of your stomach?

Spring

Inland Sea

Here, the stars bear witness,
to the spirit of this place, once
an expanse of water, its moonlit
crests sighed up. The dark shadows
of Pliosaurs and Plesiosaurs lingered,
then left. Their dull fossils now wait,
next to lustrous ribbons of opal created
from their waters, the silica
threading stories through the ground.

Seeds

In ancient soil's dark lore
they gain strength, reach
towards the unseen surface,
confident in its existence –
that the darkness will lead
to sun, that one day
they shall flourish.

Djerrinallum (Mount Elephant)

In midday light
skirts of lustrous
yellow canola billow
below, waver
in the breeze, spread
across the horizon.
A farmhouse engulfed
by yellow, a white
wood fence mirrors the
few lines of clouds.

Bees – a love letter

Sun, blinding white blossom,
blue, blue, blue sky to eternity
but your focus, your
single-minded ferocity,
is the depth
of the darkest stamen.
Bearing down, determined,
furry hind exposed to the breeze,
your primal hum reverberates,
in my chest.

                              I could reach you
                     through my kitchen window,
                  disrupt that urgent flurry -
                    but I know what you do,
                     I know how we need you,
              and I praise your urgent work -
                      you hold our survival
                  in your tiny tarsal claws.

Cinquain for Chickens

wet chicks,
soaked skinny as
spent tea bags scratch white bloom
from blown blossom, search for treats in
the squall.

Stock Crossing

put the car into park
        inhale
relax your shoulders
you've got the time
let your mind wander
if it needs to
or just focus
on the animals
before you
the herd
the hoof on the road
the low bleat
the bright blue of the sky
the flock in the distance
feel the sun's warmth
through the window
how does it make you feel?
where are you holding your tension?
      let it go
there is nowhere else to be
nowhere else to go
take a moment
release the weight behind the eyes
the herd is thinning
slowly bring your mind back
a quick wave to the stock person
on her motorbike
slide the car into drive

        namaste

Home

He wanted to make sure
that when she came home
everything was perfect,
he was doing it for her.

Go home, she'd said.
The closest cancer ward is a days drive,
and she'll be there for a while.

I'll be fine, I'm in good hands, she'd said.
He cooked a few meals and froze them.
He pulled out the mop, added too much detergent.

It makes no sense to sit idle, she'd said.
He dusted and vacuumed, found an old tin of paint
for the kitchen door.

The post office needs to function, she'd said.
He washed the sheets. And towels. He didn't touch
the photo albums that needed sorting.

It's too hard to find staff to replace you, she'd said.
He mowed the lawn, changed the oil in the car,
checked the tyres, wiped out the dust.

You're irreplaceable, she'd smiled.

He wanted to make sure
that when she came home
everything was perfect, he was doing
it for her.

The Word Search

We agree
to make a word search
for each other,

it's covid
lockdown and
we need something.

We measure
out centimetre
lines to connect,

you're newly
six and the thrill of
a fresh ruled line is euphoric.

I pluck words,
like shells on our beach walks - only
the ones that will suit you best;

our names, your
school, three-letter words
you can read alone.

You fret
about spelling, lock
away in the pantry to forge

words from
easy-to-reach packets,
and issue a frustrated squeal

when you start
'gluten free' but run out
of squares at 'f'.

You change from
pen to texta, then
realising the fatal error,

submit and
retreat to the
television.

Days later,
thoughts heavy with
newsfeeds and graphs

I find your
unfinished page,
circle through

words that aren't
listed - *Easiyo* and
Deliciouschips,

incorrect spelling,
multi-colours and backwards
'j's'. The resplendence

buoys me past
the horror of now
and to another place.

Gifts

In the low-sun briny glare,
an angry wind whips sand
into threads of hair
while she unfaltering
searches the beach
for Mother's Day presents.

Shells, cuttlefish, pearls of seaweed
lace through her tiny fingers
and into mine –
hold these, but don't look,
she yells above the squall,
serious faced, running off
to collect more bounty.

As we head for the car,
my hands laden with treasures,
she seeks something to hold
to steady her sand wobbles,
but all I can spare
is one finger.

The Secret

creeping　　　　　　tiptoed to perfect height,
　　　　　　　　　　　surging with thrill
she gently noses
the top of his ear –
thick with age.

she smells of childhood,
her hair a web against his cheek,
her breath warm on his face,

he waits.

　　　　　　　　she has selected him
and
the words pour forth,
the perfect volume
to stop overhearing.

he watches her
　　　　　　　step back,
　　　　　　　weight on her heels
waiting for his reaction
and her crumpled face breaks
his heart when he tells her,
that was my deaf ear.

Scones

he's made fucking scones

with homemade
heritage plum jam
added wattleseed to gloat
the absolute

                g a l l

walking across
the mechanics institute hall
holding out a full fucking platter
of whipped-cream clouds

his grin   that apron

he's made fucking *scones*
when he knows
full-well

that

this

is

a

lamington

drive

The C.W.A.

They make scones to perfect proportions,
no flour-drop from base to blouse,
sponges without cooling rack lines,

jams at perfect consistency, and
cookbooks with metric conversions.
They rake profits into piles,

for scholarships,
disaster and drought relief,
fight environmental causes,

want to ban fracking,
keep an eye on Aus post
and food labeling lies.

They lobby for pay parity,
an end to superannuation poverty,
rights for women and girls.

If only they could
whip up a Prime Minister
like a pav.

What would Kate Jennings do?

In memory of Kate Jennings 1948-2021

She pulls out ugly-as-fuck plastic tubs
filled with readers from a too-long-ago arts degree,
brushes off a festival of varying-in-size pest shit
and disturbs the long-forgotten-dreams from
inner-city-melbourne when she was a
soy-latte-sipper with change-the-world ambitions.
Now she needs bonfire-starter-paper, space for
kids toys-and-clothes to be locked away
between innings of newborns. She opens
the cover of introduction-to-poetry
for a bit-of-fun, flicks through the names
wordsworth-hardy-hughes.
Did she notice it in 2001?
The lack-of-women?
Even the critical articles are-all-blokes.
Something stirs, deeper-than-nostalgia, it's anger.
The feeling of fuck-those-journals
printed in the previously-published-in sections,
the by-agent-only publishers, the no-unsolicited-manuscripts,
the under-twenty-five competitions.
She remembers the thrill, the dusty-musty-books
by feminist poets in second-hand-bookshops
the wildly-passionate-voices,
the fuck-the-patriarchy approaches.

She thinks
What would Kate Jennings do?

And she takes up her pen.

Acknowledgements

This book was written on Wadawurrung and Gunditjmara Country.

I gratefully acknowledge the Traditional Custodians of the land, water and culture, the Wadawurrung and Gunditjmara People. I pay my respects to Elders past, present and emerging. I recognise their continuing custodianship of the land, water and culture. And I recognise that I, and my children, benefit from this custodianship.

Inspiration for these poems came from many places across Australia and I extend this acknowledgement to all Aboriginal and Torres Strait Islander People.

I recognise that sovereignty has never been ceded. I recognise that dispossession and genocide is part of Australia's history, and its impact is present today.

I'd like to acknowledge the support of the Ballarat Arts Foundation for awarding me a mentorship for 2021 and matching me perfectly with Gillian Schroeter who kept this project afloat through lockdown after lockdown.

I'd also like to acknowledge the poets who have provided feedback on some of these poems including Fiona Wright and members of the NSW Writer's Centre poetry workshops, and my Ballarat feedback crew, Suzanne Gatz, Nadine Craenburg, Bronwyn Blaiklock, Jess McCulloch and Megan J Reidl. This also includes Kirstyn McDermott and Jason Nurung from Words Out Loud.

Big thanks to my friends and family for supporting me in this project. A specific cheers to Adam McNicholl and Eloise Brown for the coffees and confidence boosting chats.

Thank you to my parents and siblings, nieces and nephews, steps and in-laws, and those 20 year plus friends, who've been listening to me bang on about poetry forever (you know who you are).

And, of course Ben, James, Henry & Lillian, who couldn't escape these poems in lockdown. I love you.

The following poems have been previously published:

'Mother's Day' was published in *They Are Us* 2020 and inspired a bronze statue from Abagail Robertson for the accompanying exhibition.

'How to paint a sigh' was judged Highly Commended in the Nillumbik Ekphrasis Poetry Award 2015 and published as part of the prize. It was inspired by a David Moore oil, *Untitled - (Landscape with water)*.

'George and the Vegans' was recorded for the Melbourne Spoken Word Festival podcast in 2020.

About the Author

Melissa Watts has published poetry, fiction and non-fiction. Her poems have inspired other artists to craft bronze statues and compose piano performances for audiences in New York - which is a long way from her home on Wadawurrung country, Ballarat, Australia.

Melissa has a Bachelor of Arts with Honours from the University of Melbourne and will complete a Creative Writing PhD in 2022.

Melissa is also an adult educator and facilitator who loves inspiring creatives to deepen their practice and achieve their goals.

Connect with Melissa via:
Web: www.melissawatts.net
Twitter: @MelissaAWatts
Instagram: Melissa_Watts_Writer

www.ingramcontent.com/pod-product-compliance
Lightning Source LLC
Chambersburg PA
CBHW030302010526
44107CB00053B/1786